MATH TRAILBLAZERS™

Grade 3

Unit Resource Guide
Unit 19
Multiplication and Division Problems

SECOND EDITION

A Mathematical Journey Using Science and Language Arts

KENDALL/HUNT PUBLISHING COMPANY
4050 Westmark Drive   Dubuque, Iowa 52002

A TIMS® Curriculum
University of Illinois at Chicago

UIC The University of Illinois
at Chicago

The original edition was based on work supported by the National Science Foundation under grant
No. MDR 9050226 and the University of Illinois at Chicago. Any opinions, findings, and conclusions
or recommendations expressed in this publication are those of the author(s) and do not necessarily
reflect the views of the granting agencies.

LETTER HOME

Multiplication and Division Problems

Date: _____

Dear Family Member:

In this unit, we return to the study of multiplication and division. Students solve problems involving multiplying two-digit by one-digit numbers, for example, 73×5. They also extend their division skills.

In the previous multiplication units, students developed their understanding of *what* multiplication is and *when* it can be used to solve a problem. Here, our focus is on *how* to multiply. There are three important types of computing: mental, calculator, and paper and pencil. This unit introduces a paper-and-pencil method.

The method for multiplying taught here is different from the traditional one. For example, many people solve a problem like 37×4 as shown:

$$
\begin{array}{r}
\overset{2}{37} \\
\times\ 4 \\
\hline
148
\end{array}
$$

In the method we use, every product is written down:

$$
\begin{array}{r}
37 \\
\times\ 4 \\
\hline
28 \\
+\ 120 \\
\hline
148
\end{array}
$$

$\longrightarrow$ Think "30 + 7"	Step 1
$\longleftarrow$ Multiply 4×7	Step 2
$\longleftarrow$ Multiply 4×30	Step 3
$\longleftarrow$ Add 28 + 120	Step 4

By showing each step, students further develop their understanding of the multiplication process.

Help your child at home:

- Talk about problems that come up in everyday life, for example, "If gas costs $1.20 per gallon, how much does 5 gallons cost?" or "If eggs cost 99¢ cents a dozen, about how much does one egg cost?"

- Help your child prepare for a quiz on the last six multiplication facts (4×6, 4×7, 4×8, 7×6, 8×6, 8×7) by reviewing with the *Triangle Flash Cards.*

Thank you for your continued support of your child's learning.

Sincerely,

UNIT 19 UNIT OUTLINE

Multiplication and Division Problems

Components Key: SG = Student Guide, DAB = Discovery Assignment Book, AB = Adventure Book, URG = Unit Resource Guide, and DPP = Daily Practice and Problems

	Sessions	Description	Supplies
LESSON 1 **Break-apart Products** SG pages 286–289 URG pages 19–28 DPP A–B	1	**ACTIVITY:** Students solve multiplication problems by breaking products into the sum of simpler products using rectangular arrays drawn on grid paper. They begin with multiplying one-digit numbers and move to multiplying a two-digit number by a one-digit number.	• crayons or colored pencils • red or green overhead markers
LESSON 2 **More Multiplication Stories** SG pages 290–294 URG pages 29–38 DPP C–J	4	**ACTIVITY:** Students solve problems that involve multiplying two-digit numbers by one-digit numbers, with particular attention given to partitioning numbers into tens and ones. They write stories to represent the multiplication problems and their partitions. This work leads to the conceptual development of a paper-and-pencil algorithm for multiplication.	
LESSON 3 **Making Groups** URG pages 39–44 DPP K–L	1	**ACTIVITY:** Students consider the number of groups of equal size that can be made from various numbers of objects. The groupings involve dividing numbers between 25 and 50, including many that cannot be solved just by using fact families. Particular attention is given to remainders.	• connecting cubes

	Sessions	Description	Supplies

LESSON 4

Solving Problems with Division

SG   pages 295–298
URG   pages 45–53
DPP   M–R

3

ACTIVITY: Students solve multiplication and division word problems, including some division word problems that involve remainders. They also solve challenging multistep problems whose solutions use both multiplication and division.

ASSESSMENT PAGE: *Multiplication and Division,* Unit Resource Guide, page 51.

CONNECTIONS

A current list of connections is available at www.mathtrailblazers.com. Detailed Information on software titles can be found in Section 13 of the Teacher Implementation Guide.

Software

- *Carmen Sandiego Math Detective* provides practice with math facts, estimation, ordering numbers, and word problems.
- *Ice Cream Truck* develops problem solving, money skills, and arithmetic operations.
- *Kid Pix, MacDraw,* or other drawing software allows students to illustrate stories using computers.
- *Math Arena* is a collection of math activities that reinforces many math concepts.
- *Mighty Math Calculating Crew* poses short answer questions about number operations and money skills.
- *National Library of Virtual Manipulatives* website (http://matti.usu.edu) allows students to work with manipulatives including rectangle multiplication that models the all-partials algorithm.

Multiplication and Division Problems

In this unit, the last of four multiplication and division units, students solve problems involving multiplication of two-digit by one-digit numbers and division problems that cannot be solved just by using fact families. They solve multiplication problems by breaking products into the sums of simpler products and write stories that represent their arithmetical processes in a meaningful way. This work leads to the conceptual development of a paper-and-pencil algorithm for the multiplication of two-digit by one-digit numbers. Students solve division problems that deal with remainders in various ways and multistep problems that involve both multiplication and division.

Distributive Law of Multiplication over Addition

In Lesson 1 *Break-apart Products,* students solve multiplication problems by breaking products into the sum of simpler products. For example, 7×4 can be broken into $5 \times 4 + 2 \times 4$. The fundamental property that is involved in this process is the **distributive property of multiplication over addition** (although students do not study this formally). This property states that for any numbers *a, b,* and *c,*

$$(a + b) \times c = (a \times c) + (b \times c)$$

To find 7×4 as expressed above, we partition 7 into two parts, $7 = 5 + 2$, and apply the distributive property with $a = 5$, $b = 2$, and $c = 4$.

The unit does not include formal instruction on the distributive property. However, the activities in this unit will help students to develop an informal understanding of this property. This type of informal understanding is very important as it enables students to do many calculations mentally and is the basis for the traditional paper-and-pencil multiplication algorithm.

Division with and without Remainders

This unit introduces no formal algorithm for division. Students are encouraged to use a variety of strategies for solving division problems with and without remainders. Strategies such as repeated subtraction, manipulative models, and calculators are emphasized, but students should be allowed to explore others. Students learn paper-and-pencil methods for division in fourth and fifth grades.

Types of Computing

Students should become proficient at all three types of computing: mental, calculator, and paper and pencil. They should also develop a sense of when each of these methods is appropriate. Furthermore, they should be able to make estimations as well as use each method to find exact answers. This unit develops a paper-and-pencil algorithm for multiplication, but students can also practice other types of computing. They can use mental math to make estimates to verify the reasonableness of their answers, and they can use calculators to check their exact answers.

This unit introduces students to the all-partials algorithm for multiplication. This algorithm is different from the compact algorithm in that it allows students to write all partial products. The lesson guide for Lesson 2 *More Multiplication Stories* discusses this algorithm. You can refer to the TIMS Tutor: *Arithmetic* in the *Teacher Implementation Guide* for more information regarding algorithms. Though we focus on the all-partials algorithm, students should not be discouraged from using other correct paper-and-pencil algorithms that make sense to them.

Resources

- Fuson, K.C. "Developing Mathematical Power in Whole Number Operations." In *A Research Companion to Principles and Standards for School Mathematics.* J. Kilpatrick, W.G. Martin, and D. Schifter, eds. National Council of Teachers of Mathematics, Reston, VA, 2003.
- Lampert, M. "Teaching Multiplication." *Journal of Mathematical Behavior.* Volume 5, Norwood, NJ, pages 241–280, 1986.
- National Research Council. "Developing Proficiency with Whole Numbers." In *Adding It Up: Helping Children Learn Mathematics.* J. Kilpatrick, J. Swafford, and B. Findell, eds. National Academy Press, Washington, DC, 2001.
- *Principles and Standards for School Mathematics.* National Council of Teachers of Mathematics, Reston, VA, 2000.

Assessment Indicators

- Can students represent 2-digit by 1-digit multiplication problems using manipulatives, arrays, and drawings?
- Can students solve 2-digit by 1-digit multiplication problems using manipulatives, arrays, and drawings?
- Can students multiply numbers with ending zeros?
- Can students write number sentences for multiplication and division situations?
- Can students create stories for multiplication and division sentences?
- Can students solve multiplication and division problems and explain their reasoning?
- Can students interpret remainders?
- Do students demonstrate fluency with the multiplication facts for the last six facts (4×6, 4×7, 4×8, 6×7, 6×8, 7×8)?

OBSERVATIONAL ASSESSMENT RECORD

(A1) Can students represent 2-digit by 1-digit multiplication problems using manipulatives, arrays, and drawings?

(A2) Can students solve 2-digit by 1-digit multiplication problems using manipulatives, arrays, and drawings?

(A3) Can students multiply numbers with ending zeros?

(A4) Can students write number sentences for multiplication and division situations?

(A5) Can students create stories for multiplication and division sentences?

(A6) Can students solve multiplication and division problems and explain their reasoning?

(A7) Can students interpret remainders?

(A8) Do students demonstrate fluency with the multiplication facts for the last six facts $(4 \times 6, 4 \times 7, 4 \times 8, 6 \times 7, 6 \times 8, 7 \times 8)$?

(A9) _____

Name	A1	A2	A3	A4	A5	A6	A7	A8	A9	Comments
1.										
2.										
3.										
4.										
5.										
6.										
7.										
8.										
9.										
10.										
11.										
12.										
13.										

Name	A1	A2	A3	A4	A5	A6	A7	A8	A9	Comments
14.										
15.										
16.										
17.										
18.										
19.										
20.										
21.										
22.										
23.										
24.										
25.										
26.										
27.										
28.										
29.										
30.										
31.										
32.										

Daily Practice and Problems

Multiplication and Division Problems

Two Daily Practice and Problems (DPP) items are included for each class session listed in the Unit Outline. A Scope and Sequence Chart for the DPP can be found in the *Teacher Implementation Guide*.

A DPP Menu for Unit 19

Icons in the Teacher Notes column designate the subject matter of each DPP item. The first item for each class session is always a Bit and the second is either a Task or Challenge. Each item falls into one or more of the categories listed below. A menu of the DPP items for Unit 19 follows.

N **Number Sense**	**Computation**	**Time**	**Geometry**
D, F–I, K, P	C, D, F–I, L, N, O, R	M	B, J, P
Math Facts	**$** **Money**	**Measurement**	**Data**
A, E, H, K, P, Q	C, F, I, R	B	

Practicing and Assessing the Multiplication Facts

In Unit 11, students began the systematic, strategies-based study of the multiplication facts. In Unit 19, students review and practice the multiplication facts for the last six facts: 4×6, 4×7, 4×8, 6×7, 6×8, 7×8. The *Triangle Flash Cards* for these groups were distributed in Unit 15 in the *Discovery Assignment Book* immediately following the Home Practice. They can also be found in the Generic Section of the *Unit Resource Guide*. In Unit 19,

DPP items A, E, H, K, and P provide practice with multiplication facts for these groups. Bit Q is the *Multiplication Quiz: Last Six Facts*. Students will take an inventory test on all the facts in Unit 20.

For information on the distribution and study of the multiplication facts in Grade 3, see the DPP Guide for Units 3 and 11. For a detailed explanation of our approach to learning and assessing the math facts in Grade 3 see the *Grade 3 Facts Resource Guide* and for information for Grades K–5, see the TIMS Tutor: *Math Facts* in the *Teacher Implementation Guide*.

Students may solve the items individually, in groups, or as a class. The items may also be assigned for homework.

Student Questions	Teacher Notes

 Facts: The Last Six Facts

A. $4 \times 8 =$ B. $4 \times 7 =$

C. $7 \times 6 =$ D. $4 \times 6 =$

E. $8 \times 6 =$ F. $8 \times 7 =$

Explain your strategy for Question C.

TIMS Bit

Discuss strategies students use to solve the facts, emphasizing those strategies that are more efficient than others. For example, to solve 7×6, students might double the answer to 7×3. Similarly, students may use doubling to solve facts for 4s. For example, to solve 4×6, students might double 6 to get 12 and then double 12 to get 24. Using break-apart facts is a possible strategy, but may not be efficient for some—$8 \times 7 = 8 \times 5 + 8 \times 2$ or $40 + 16 = 56$. Students may also say, "I just know it." Recall is obviously an efficient strategy.

Students should take home the *Triangle Flash Cards: The Last Six Facts* to study at home with a family member. Tell students when the quiz on this group of facts will be given. DPP Bit Q is *Multiplication Quiz: Last Six Facts*.

Student Questions	Teacher Notes

 Cube Model Plans

Use the cube model plan below to find the following:

1. volume of the model

2. height of the model

3. area of floor

You may build the cube model with connecting cubes if it helps.

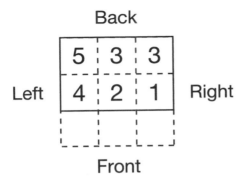

Back

5	3	3
4	2	1

Left   Right

Front

TIMS Task

Be sure that students use appropriate units when expressing their answers.

1. 18 cubic units

2. 5 units

3. 6 square units

 Adding and Subtracting Money

Complete the following problems. Use pencil and paper or mental math to find the answers.

1. $2.45 − $1.05 =

2. $7.60 + $9.95 =

3. $6.75 − $ .32 =

4. $5.99 + $4.25 =

5. Explain a way to solve Question 4 using mental math.

TIMS Bit

1. $1.40
2. $17.55
3. $6.43
4. $10.24
5. Possible strategy: students may replace $5.99 with $6 and easily add the $4.25. Then they could subtract the last penny for an answer of $10.24.

Multiplication Story $8 \times \frac{1}{4}$

Write a story and draw a picture about $8 \times \frac{1}{4}$.

Write a number sentence on your picture.

TIMS Task

2; Students can share their stories with the class.

 Multiplication Table

Fill in the missing information on this multiplication table.

×	4	6	7	8
4				
6				
7				
8				

TIMS Bit

Discuss the strategies students used to complete the multiplication chart. Focus attention on how students solved the last six facts. (4×8, 4×7, 4×6, 7×6, 8×6, and 8×7)

F Making Change

Beth asked for her allowance of $1.70 in nickels and dimes. Her parents gave her $1.00 using one kind of coin and $.70 using the other coin.

1. How many nickels did Beth possibly get? How many dimes?

2. Beth said, "I wanted the same number of nickels as dimes." Is this possible? If so, how many nickels? How many dimes? If not, why?

TIMS Challenge

1. 20 nickels and 7 dimes or 10 dimes and 14 nickels

2. No; 10 nickels is $.50 and 10 dimes is $1.00: $1.50

   12 nickels is $.60 and 12 dimes is $1.20: $1.80

   11 nickels is $.55 and 11 dimes is $1.10: $1.65

G Using Doubles

Solve these problems in your head. Write only the answers. Be ready to explain your answers.

1. 7 + 7 =   2. 7 + 6 =

3. 8 + 7 =   4. 80 + 80 =

5. 90 + 80 =   6. 80 + 85 =

7. 30 + 30 =   8. 30 + 32 =

9. 30 + 25 =

TIMS Bit

1. 14   2. 13

3. 15   4. 160

5. 170   6. 165

7. 60   8. 62

9. 55

These problems are grouped together to encourage students to use doubles to find the answers. For example, 80 + 85 can be solved by doubling 80 and adding 5 (80 + 80 + 5).

Skip Counting

1. Skip count by 4s to 100. Say the numbers quietly to yourself. Write the numbers.

2. Skip count by 8s until you pass 100. Say the numbers quietly to yourself. Write the numbers.

3. Circle the numbers in your lists that are products of (answers to) the last six facts:

   4×6 4×7 4×8

   6×7 6×8 7×8

4. How could you use skip counting to find these facts?

5. Which of the last six facts is not circled? Why not?

TIMS Task

1–2. If your calculator has the constant feature, press $4 + 4 = = = = = = = =$. Each time = is pressed, the constant number (4) and the constant operation (addition) is repeated. Some students may find it helpful to count by twos, accentuating every other number: 2, <u>4</u>, 6, <u>8</u>, 10, <u>12</u>, 14, <u>16</u>, etc. Then, count by 8s.

Have students write down the numbers as they count. Discuss patterns in the two lists.

3. Students circle 24, 28, 32, 48, and 56 in both lists.

4. Answers will vary. To find 4×8, students can skip count by 4, eight times: 4, 8, 12, 16, 24, 28, ㉜

5. $6 \times 7 = 42$; 42 is not a multiple of 4.

 Lizardland

Use the picture of Lizardland in your *Student Guide* from Unit 11.

1. Sam wants 2 hot dogs. What will it cost?

2. Sam agrees to treat Adam to 2 hot dogs. How much will 4 hot dogs cost?

3. Tim spent $12 trying to win the Lizard stuffed animal. How many hot dogs could he have bought with the $12?

TIMS Bit

Discuss patterns in these problems. How can doubling help? Discuss strategies used to solve the problems. The sign for Lizard Lunch in the picture of Lizardland shows that one hot dog costs $1.50.

1. $3.00

2. $6.00

3. 8 hot dogs

Student Questions	Teacher Notes

 Squares and Rectangles

1. Draw a square. Then, write what a square is.

2. Draw a rectangle. Then, write what a rectangle is.

3. What is the difference between squares and rectangles?

4. Is a square a rectangle?

5. Is a rectangle a square?

TIMS Task

1. A square is a four-sided figure with four right angles and four equal sides. It is a special kind of rectangle.

2. A rectangle is a four-sided figure with four right angles. Opposite sides are parallel and the same length.

3. Students should identify the similarities between the square and the rectangle such as both have four sides and right angles, and opposite sides are the same length. The only difference is that a square's four sides are all the same length.

4. Yes

5. Not always

 Double, Double Again

Solve the following problems.

1. $6 \times 2 =$ 2. $6 \times 4 =$

3. $8 \times 2 =$ 4. $8 \times 4 =$

5. $7 \times 2 =$ 6. $14 \times 2 =$

7. $7 \times 4 =$ 8. $14 \times 4 =$

9. $7 \times 8 =$

TIMS Bit

The first four are from students' multiplication tables. Discuss the patterns and answers before assigning Questions 5–9.

1. 12   2. 24

3. 16   4. 32

5. 14   6. 28

7. 28   8. 56

9. 56

Multiplication Story 38 × 4

Solve 38 × 4. Write a story and draw a picture to match your solution.

TIMS Task

152

Stories and pictures will vary.

 Today, Tonight, or Tomorrow?

1. What time will it be 4 hours from now?

2. What time will it be $6\frac{1}{3}$ hours from now?

3. What time will it be 8 hours from now?

4. What time will it be $12\frac{1}{4}$ hours from now?

TIMS Bit

Work with a clock, showing the position of the minute hand as students count.

Mathhoppers on the Calculator

1. A +9 mathhopper starts at 2 and hops 15 times. Estimate where it lands.

2. Where does it land exactly? Tell how you know.

3. How many more hops does it need to take to reach 200?

TIMS Challenge

1. Accept a wide range of estimates. One possibility is to think of a +10 mathhopper hopping 15 times. The +9 mathhopper will then land around 150.

2. 137; Possible keystrokes: 15 × 9 + 2 =

3. 7 more hops; Students may skip count by 9 on the calculator from 137 to 200. Another possibility is to subtract: 200 − 137 = 63. The mathhopper must hop over 63 more numbers. 63 ÷ 9 = 7 hops

Student Questions	Teacher Notes

 Some More Sums

Add 27 to each of the numbers below.

| 65 | 189 | 2977 |

TIMS Bit

Students may use base-ten pieces or paper and pencil to find the answers.

| 92 | 216 | 3004 |

 Rectangles and Products

1. Using *Centimeter Grid Paper,* draw all the rectangles you can make with 32 tiles.

2. Draw all the rectangles you can make with 24 tiles.

TIMS Task

Distribute *Centimeter Grid Paper. Centimeter Grid Paper* is available in the Generic Section. Have students draw rectangles that can be formed using tiles.

1. 4 cm by 8 cm
   2 cm by 16 cm
   1 cm by 32 cm (will not fit on grid paper)

2. 6 cm by 4 cm
   8 cm by 3 cm
   12 cm by 2 cm
   24 cm by 1 cm (will not fit on grid paper)

 **Multiplication Quiz: The Last Six Facts**

A. $8 \times 6 =$	B. $6 \times 4 =$
C. $4 \times 7 =$	D. $7 \times 8 =$
E. $6 \times 7 =$	F. $8 \times 4 =$

TIMS Bit

This quiz is on the fifth and final group of multiplication facts, the last six facts. We recommend 1 minute for this quiz. Allow students to change pens after the time is up and complete the remaining problems in a different color.

After students take the test, have them update their *Multiplication Facts I Know* charts.

Saturday at Lizardland

Use the Lizardland picture in your *Student Guide* from Unit 11 to solve the following problems.

1. On Saturday, in the first hour, 100 adults and 200 children came to Lizardland. How much was collected in ticket sales?

2. Last Saturday 600 adults and 1000 children came to Lizardland. How much was collected in ticket sales?

3. Fifty-nine members of the Jones family reunion came to Lizardland on Saturday. Forty-four family members were children. Fifteen were adults. How much did they pay to get in?

TIMS Task

The admission sign at the entrance to Lizardland in the *Student Guide* lists the adult price (on Saturday) of $6.00 and the children's price of $3.00.

1. $600 + $600 = $1200

2. $3600 + $3000 = $6600

3. 44 × $3 + 15 × $6 = $222

LESSON GUIDE

Break-apart Products

Estimated Class Sessions:
1

Students break products, such as 6×8, into the sum of simpler products, e.g., $6 \times 5 + 6 \times 3$. To do this, they draw a rectangular array on grid paper to represent a product, divide the array into two smaller arrays that represent easier products, and add the easier products to get their answers. They begin with one-digit by one-digit problems and move to two-digit by one-digit problems. In doing this activity, students develop an understanding of the distributive property of multiplication over addition although they do not study it formally.

Key Content

- Representing multiplication problems using arrays.
- Solving multiplication problems by writing them as the sum of easier problems.
- Writing number sentences for multiplication situations.
- Solving multiplication problems and explaining the reasoning.
- Multiplying numbers with ending zeros.

Daily Practice and Problems: Bit for Lesson 1

A. Facts: The Last Six Facts (URG p. 10)

A. $4 \times 8 =$	B. $4 \times 7 =$
C. $7 \times 6 =$	D. $4 \times 6 =$
E. $8 \times 6 =$	F. $8 \times 7 =$

Explain your strategy for Question C.

DPP Task is on page 22. Suggestions for using the DPPs are on page 22.

Curriculum Sequence

Before This Unit

Multiplication. Students developed multiplication concepts in Grade 3 Units 3, 7, and 11. They began a systematic study of the multiplication facts in Unit 11 and continued the practice and assessment of the multiplication facts in the Daily Practice and Problems in Units 12–19.

Materials List

Print Materials for Students

	Math Facts and Daily Practice and Problems	Activity	Homework
Student Books — Student Guide		*Break-apart Products* Pages 286–288	*Break-apart Products* Homework Section Pages 288–289
Student Books — Discovery Assignment Book			Home Practice Part 1 Page 268
Teacher Resources — Facts Resource Guide ◎	DPP Item 19A Use *Triangle Flash Cards: The Last Six Facts* to review the multiplication facts for this group.		
Teacher Resources — Unit Resource Guide ◎	DPP Items A–B Pages 10–11		
Teacher Resources — Generic Section ◎		*Centimeter Grid Paper,* 5–6 per student and *Small Multiplication Tables,* 1 table per student	*Triangle Flash Cards: The Last Six Facts,* 1 per student (optional)

◎ *available on Teacher Resource CD*

All Transparency Masters, Blackline Masters, and Assessment Blackline Masters in the Unit Resource Guide are on the Teacher Resource CD.

Supplies for Each Student

crayons or colored pencils

Materials for the Teacher

Rectangular Arrays Transparency Master (Unit Resource Guide) Page 25
red and green overhead markers

Developing the Activity

Show students Rectangle A on the *Rectangular Arrays* Transparency Master. The 7 × 4 rectangle represents the product 7 × 4. Color in the rectangle so that a 5 × 4 rectangle is red and a 2 × 4 rectangle is green, showing that 7 × 4 = 5 × 4 + 2 × 4. Students can follow along with the example in the *Break-apart Products* Activity Pages in the *Student Guide* (See Figure 1). Use the following discussion prompts:

- *How many square centimeters are in this rectangle?* (7 × 4 = 28 sq cm)

- *How many square centimeters are in the red and green regions?* (5 × 4 = 20 sq cm and 2 × 4 = 8 sq cm)

- *This picture shows a way to solve 7 × 4. What is a number sentence that describes that way?* (7 × 4 = 5 × 4 + 2 × 4)

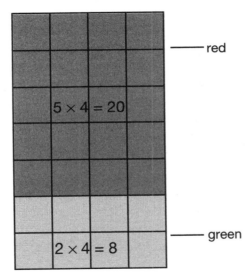

Figure 1: *Rectangle A showing that 7 × 4 = 5 × 4 + 2 × 4*

Another way to solve 7 × 4, illustrated in Figure 2, is to break apart the 4 into 2 + 2. You can wipe off your shading on the transparency of Rectangle A and illustrate this second way of solving 7 × 4.

$$
\begin{aligned}
7 \times 4 &= 7 \times 2 + 7 \times 2 \\
&= 14 + 14 \\
&= 28
\end{aligned}
$$

Break-apart Products

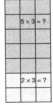

One way to solve a multiplication problem is to break it apart into easier problems.

Example: Find 7 × 4.

Look at this 7 × 4 rectangle.

There are 5 × 4 = 20 red squares and 2 × 4 = 8 green squares.

So, 7 × 4 = 5 × 4 + 2 × 4
= 20 + 8
= 28

1. On a separate sheet of grid paper, draw a 7 × 3 rectangle.
   A. Color the first 5 rows red.
      Complete: 5 × 3 = ?
   B. Color the last 2 rows green.
      Complete: 2 × 3 = ?
   C. Complete these number sentences for your rectangle.
      7 × 3 = ? × 3 + ? × 3
      7 × 3 = ? + ?
      = ?

Student Guide - Page 286

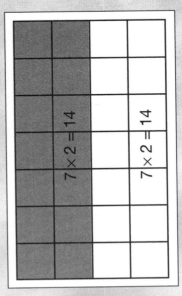

Figure 2: *Rectangle A showing that 7 × 4 = 7 × 2 + 7 × 2*

2. Draw a 6 × 8 rectangle on grid paper.
   A. Color the first 5 rows red. How many squares are red? Finish this number sentence: 5 × 8 = ?
   B. Color the last row green. How many squares are green? Write a number sentence for this part.
   C. How much is 6 × 8? Use these number sentences to help you.
   6 × 8 = ? × 8 + ? × 8
   6 × 8 =   ? + ?
          =   ?

5 × 8 = ?

1 × 8 = ?

3. Draw a 3 × 8 rectangle horizontally on your grid paper.
   A. Color the top two rows red.
   B. Color the bottom row green.
   C. Complete: 3 × 8 = ? + ?
                         = ?

4. Draw rectangles of the following sizes. As in Questions 1–3, break each rectangle into two pieces by coloring. Then, compute the answer using easier products. Write number sentences beside your rectangles to show your answers.
   A. 7 × 8   **B.** 9 × 6

5. Use rectangles to help solve the following problems. Write number sentences beside your rectangles.
   A. 3 × 12   **B.** 4 × 15   **C.** 2 × 17

Break-apart Products   SG · Grade 3 · Unit 19 · Lesson 1   *287*

Student Guide - Page 287

Daily Practice and Problems:
Task for Lesson 1

B. Task: Cube Model Plans
   (URG p. 11)

Use the cube model plan below to find the following:

1. volume of the model

2. height of the model

3. area of floor

You may build the cube model with connecting cubes if it helps.

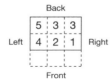

Back

| 5 | 3 | 3 |
Left | 4 | 2 | 1 | Right

Front

The rectangles on the *Rectangular Arrays* transparency can be used to discuss ways to solve the following problems:

   A. 7 × 4
   B. 4 × 8
   C. 12 × 9
   D. 17 × 3

Encourage students to break apart the products in ways that provide easier products. The example in Figure 1 involves a multiple of 5, which is probably easier for most students than the original multiple of 7. On the other hand, breaking 7 × 4 into 3 × 4 + 4 × 4 might not be much easier.

Products that have at least one factor between 10 and 20, such as problems C and D, can be broken apart so that one of the easier products involves 10. For D, students can break apart the product in this way: 17 × 3 = 10 × 3 + 7 × 3. Again, point out that it is helpful to break numbers into products that are easier. Breaking 17 × 3 into 13 × 3 + 4 × 3 is correct, but probably not any easier to solve.

After you have worked together to break apart several products, ask students to solve *Questions 1–6* on the *Break-apart Products* Activity Pages. They will use grid paper for all of the in-class problems.

Breaking apart products allows students to do many calculations mentally and is, in fact, the basis for the traditional paper-and-pencil multiplication algorithm. The fundamental property that is involved in breaking apart products is the distributive property of multiplication over addition. (See the Background section of this unit.) Informal understanding of this property is very important for students; however, formal study at this stage is not necessary.

Suggestions for Teaching the Lesson

Math Facts

DPP Bit A provides practice with the last six multiplication facts in preparation for the quiz in this unit.

Homework and Practice

- DPP Task B asks students to use a cube model plan to find the area, volume, and height of a three-dimensional shape.

- Remind students to take home their *Triangle Flash Cards: The Last Six Facts* to prepare for the quiz in DPP Bit Q.

- Students will need two or three copies of *Centimeter Grid Paper* to solve the problems in the Homework section of the *Student Guide.* Homework *Questions 1–8* provide more examples of two-digit by one-digit multiplication. *Questions 9–20* provide practice with multiplication by tens which will be helpful for the next lesson. Have students take home a *Small Multiplication Table* from the Generic Section to help them find needed multiplication facts. *Questions 1* and *2* of the Homework section present an opportunity to discuss solutions that are more efficient than others.

- Home Practice Part 1 asks students to estimate sums using benchmarks.

Answers for Part 1 of the Home Practice can be found in the Answer Key at the end of this lesson and at the end of this unit.

Assessment

Questions 3–6 in the Homework section can be used to assess students' abilities to represent and solve 2-digit by 1-digit multiplication problems using drawings. Students will need two copies of *Centimeter Grid Paper.* *Questions 9–20* of the Homework section can be used to assess students' abilities to multiply numbers with ending zeros.

Discovery Assignment Book - Page 268

---

6. Rachel found 5 × 12 by breaking the 12 apart. One part was a 10.

$5 \times 12 = 5 \times 10 + 5 \times 2$

$= 50 \ + \ 10$

$= 60$

Ben found 5 × 12 by breaking the 12 into two equal parts:

$5 \times 12 = 5 \times 6 + 5 \times 6$

$= 30 \ + \ 30$

$= 60$

Solve the following problems by breaking them apart. Use Rachel's method at least twice, and use Ben's method at least twice.

A. 5 × 18 = ?	B. 16 × 3 = ?
C. 6 × 14 = ?	D. 4 × 23 = ?
E. 13 × 4 = ?	F. 2 × 36 = ?

Homework

You will need *Centimeter Grid Paper* to complete this homework.

Hannah broke apart a rectangle to find 12 × 4. Her solution is shown below.

There are 8 × 4 = 32 green squares and 4 × 4 = 16 red squares.

So, $12 \times 4 = 8 \times 4 + 4 \times 4$

$= 32 \ + \ 16$

$= 48$

1. On a separate sheet of *Centimeter Grid Paper* draw a 12 × 4 rectangle. Use this rectangle to show a different method than Hannah's. Write number sentences beside your rectangle to show your answer.

Student Guide - Page 288

---

2. Draw two 14 × 4 rectangles on a sheet of *Centimeter Grid Paper.* Find 14 × 4 by breaking the rectangles apart. Show two different methods. Write number sentences beside your rectangles to show your answers.

Find the following products by breaking them apart into simpler products. Use *Centimeter Grid Paper* to help you.

3. 5 × 12	4. 2 × 15	5. 5 × 24
6. 14 × 3	7. 9 × 6	8. 3 × 13

Review

Find the following products any way you like. You do not have to use the break-apart method. You may use your multiplication table to help you.

9. 10 × 4	10. 7 × 20
11. 3 × 60	12. 5 × 70
13. 9 × 30	14. 8 × 20
15. 4 × 40	16. 6 × 80
17. 7 × 90	18. 5 × 80
19. 9 × 40	20. 3 × 50

Student Guide - Page 289

AT A GLANCE

Math Facts and Daily Practice and Problems

DPP Bit A provides practice with the last six multiplication facts. Task B asks students to find volume, floor area, and height of a three-dimensional shape.

Developing the Activity

1. Color Rectangle A on the *Rectangular Arrays* transparency to find the product 7 × 4. Then do it a second way.
2. Discuss different ways to solve problems A–D on the transparency by coloring rectangular arrays.
3. Students use grid paper to solve *Questions 1–6* from the *Break-apart Products* Activity Pages.

Homework

1. Assign Home Practice Part 1.
2. Assign *Questions 1–20* in the Homework section of the *Student Guide*.
3. Remind students to practice the last six multiplication facts using the appropriate set of *Triangle Flash Cards*.

Notes:

Rectangular Arrays

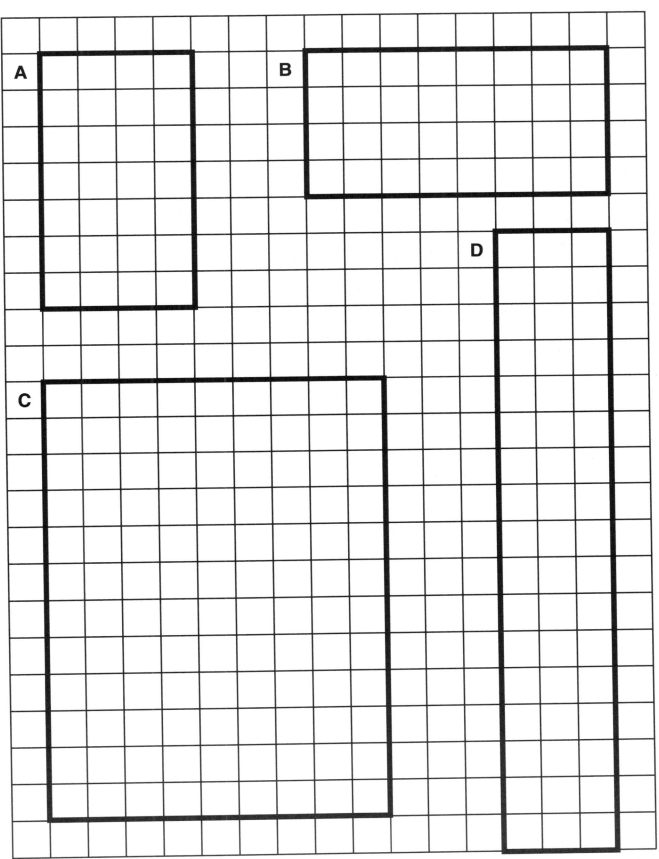

Student Guide

Questions 1–6 (SG pp. 286–288)

1.

   A. 15
   B. 6
   C. $7 \times 3 = 5 \times 3 + 2 \times 3$
   $7 \times 3 = 15 + 6$
   $ = 21$

2.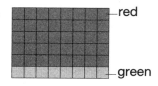

   A. 40 squares, $5 \times 8 = 40$
   B. 8 squares, $1 \times 8 = 8$
   C. $6 \times 8 = 5 \times 8 + 1 \times 8$
   $6 \times 8 = 40 + 8$
   $ = 48$

3A.–B.

   C. $3 \times 8 = 16 + 8 = 24$

4. Solution strategies may vary. One possible strategy is shown for each.

   A.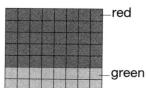

   $7 \times 8 = 5 \times 8 + 2 \times 8$
   $7 \times 8 = 40 + 16$
   $ = 56$

   B.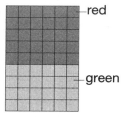

   $9 \times 6 = 5 \times 6 + 4 \times 6$
   $9 \times 6 = 30 + 24$
   $ = 54$

5. Solution strategies may vary. One possible strategy is shown.

   A.

   $3 \times 12 = 3 \times 10 + 3 \times 2$
   $3 \times 12 = 30 + 6$
   $ = 36$

   B.

   $4 \times 15 = 4 \times 10 + 4 \times 5$
   $4 \times 15 = 40 + 20$
   $ = 60$

   C.

   $2 \times 17 = 2 \times 10 + 2 \times 7$
   $2 \times 17 = 20 + 14$
   $ = 34$

*Answers and/or discussion are included in the Lesson Guide.
**Answers for all the Home Practice in the *Discovery Assignment Book* are at the end of the unit.

26 URG • Grade 3 • Unit 19 • Lesson 1 • Answer Key

6. Using Rachel's method:

A. $5 \times 18 = 5 \times 10 + 5 \times 8$
$5 \times 18 = \quad 50 \quad + \quad 40$
$\quad\quad\quad = \quad 90$

B. $16 \times 3 = 10 \times 3 + 6 \times 3$
$16 \times 3 = \quad 30 \quad + \quad 18$
$\quad\quad\quad = \quad 48$

C. $6 \times 14 = 6 \times 10 + 6 \times 4$
$6 \times 14 = \quad 60 \quad + \quad 24$
$\quad\quad\quad = \quad 84$

D. $4 \times 23 = 4 \times 20 + 4 \times 3$
$4 \times 23 = \quad 80 \quad + \quad 12$
$\quad\quad\quad = \quad 92$

E. $13 \times 4 = 10 \times 4 + 3 \times 4$
$13 \times 4 = \quad 40 \quad + \quad 12$
$\quad\quad\quad = \quad 52$

F. $2 \times 36 = 2 \times 30 + 2 \times 6$
$2 \times 36 = \quad 60 \quad + \quad 12$
$\quad\quad\quad = \quad 72$

Using Ben's method:

A. $5 \times 18 = 5 \times 9 + 5 \times 9$
$5 \times 18 = \quad 45 \quad + \quad 45$
$\quad\quad\quad = \quad 90$

B. $16 \times 3 = 8 \times 3 + 8 \times 3$
$16 \times 3 = \quad 24 \quad + \quad 24$
$\quad\quad\quad = \quad 48$

C. $6 \times 14 = 6 \times 7 + 6 \times 7$
$6 \times 14 = \quad 42 \quad + \quad 42$
$\quad\quad\quad = \quad 84$

D. $4 \times 23 = 2 \times 23 + 2 \times 23$
$4 \times 23 = \quad 46 \quad + \quad 46$
$\quad\quad\quad = \quad 92$

E. $13 \times 4 = 13 \times 2 + 13 \times 2$
$13 \times 4 = \quad 26 \quad + \quad 26$
$\quad\quad\quad = \quad 52$

F. $2 \times 36 = 2 \times 18 + 2 \times 18$
$2 \times 36 = \quad 36 \quad + \quad 36$
$\quad\quad\quad = \quad 72$

Homework (SG pp. 288–289)

Questions 1–20

Solution strategies may vary.

1. Possible answer:

$12 \times 4 = 10 \times 4 + 2 \times 4$
$12 \times 4 = \quad 40 \quad + \quad 8$
$\quad\quad\quad = \quad 48$

2. Answers may vary. Possible solutions

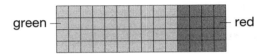

$14 \times 4 = 10 \times 4 + 4 \times 4$
$14 \times 4 = \quad 40 \quad + \quad 16$
$\quad\quad\quad = \quad 56$

$14 \times 4 = 14 \times 2 + 14 \times 2$
$\quad\quad\quad = \quad 28 \quad + \quad 28$
$\quad\quad\quad = \quad 56$

3. $5 \times 12 = 5 \times 6 + 5 \times 6$
$5 \times 12 = \quad 30 \quad + \quad 30$
$\quad\quad\quad = \quad 60$

4. $2 \times 15 = 2 \times 10 + 2 \times 5$
$2 \times 15 = \quad 20 \quad + \quad 10$
$\quad\quad\quad = \quad 30$

5. $5 \times 24 = 5 \times 20 + 5 \times 4$
$5 \times 24 = \quad 100 \quad + \quad 20$
$\quad\quad\quad = \quad 120$

6. $14 \times 3 = 10 \times 3 + 4 \times 3$
$14 \times 3 = \quad 30 \quad + \quad 12$
$\quad\quad\quad = \quad 42$

7. $9 \times 6 = 9 \times 3 + 9 \times 3$
$9 \times 6 = \quad 27 \quad + \quad 27$
$\quad\quad\quad = \quad 54$

8. $3 \times 13 = 3 \times 10 + 3 \times 3$
$3 \times 13 = \quad 30 \quad + \quad 9$
$\quad\quad\quad = \quad 39$

*Answers and/or discussion are included in the Lesson Guide.
**Answers for all the Home Practice in the *Discovery Assignment Book* are at the end of the unit.

9. 40
10. 140
11. 180
12. 350
13. 270
14. 160
15. 160
16. 480
17. 630
18. 400
19. 360
20. 150

Discovery Assignment Book

**Home Practice (DAB p. 268)

Part 1

Questions 1–9

1. equal
2. less than
3. less than
4. more than
5. equal
6. more than
7. Answers will vary. One example is
   $400 + 300 + 300 = 1000$
8. Answers will vary. One example is
   $350 + 150 + 500 = 1000$
9. Answers will vary. One example is
   $335 + 165 + 500 = 1000$

*Answers and/or discussion are included in the Lesson Guide.
**Answers for all the Home Practice in the *Discovery Assignment Book* are at the end of the unit.

LESSON GUIDE

More Multiplication Stories

Estimated Class Sessions: 4

Students solve two-digit by one-digit multiplication problems. After exploring and discussing their own methods of solving these problems, students focus on the method of breaking apart products into the sum of simpler products, with particular attention given to partitioning numbers into tens and ones. They write stories to represent the multiplication problems and then refine the stories to reflect their partitions. This work leads to the development of a paper-and-pencil algorithm.

Key Content

- Breaking products into the sum of simpler products (applying the distributive law of multiplication over addition).
- Creating stories for multiplication situations.
- Solving 2-digit by 1-digit multiplication problems using drawings and paper and pencil.

Key Vocabulary

partition

Curriculum Sequence

Before This Unit

Multiplication Stories. Students wrote multiplication stories and drew pictures for single-digit multiplication problems in Grade 3 Unit 3 Lesson 3.

Daily Practice and Problems:
Bits for Lesson 2

C. Adding and Subtracting Money
(URG p. 11)

Complete the following problems. Use pencil and paper or mental math to find the answers.

1. $2.45 − $1.05 =
2. $7.60 + $9.95 =
3. $6.75 − $ .32 =
4. $5.99 + $4.25 =
5. Explain a way to solve Question 4 using mental math.

E. Multiplication Table (URG p. 12)

Fill in the missing information on this multiplication table.

×	4	6	7	8
4				
6				
7				
8				

G. Using Doubles (URG p. 13)

Solve these problems in your head. Write only the answers. Be ready to explain your answers.

1. 7 + 7 =   2. 7 + 6 =

3. 8 + 7 =   4. 80 + 80 =

5. 90 + 80 =   6. 80 + 85 =

7. 30 + 30 =   8. 30 + 32 =

9. 30 + 25 =

I. Lizardland (URG p. 14)

Use the picture of Lizardland in your *Student Guide* from Unit 11.

1. Sam wants 2 hot dogs. What will it cost?

2. Sam agrees to treat Adam to 2 hot dogs. How much will 4 hot dogs cost?

3. Tim spent $12 trying to win the Lizard stuffed animal. How many hot dogs could he have bought with the $12?

DPP Tasks and Challenge are on page 35. Suggestions for using the DPPs are on page 35.

Materials List

Print Materials for Students

	Math Facts and Daily Practice and Problems	Activity	Homework
Student Books			
Student Guide		*More Multiplication Stories* Pages 290–294	*More Multiplication Stories* Homework Section Page 294
Discovery Assignment Book			Home Practice Part 2 Page 268
Teacher Resources			
Facts Resource Guide ⊙	DPP Items 19E & 19H		
Unit Resource Guide ⊙	DPP Items C–J Pages 11–15		
Generic Section ⊙		*Small Multiplication Tables,* 1 table per student (optional)	

⊙ *available on Teacher Resource CD*

All Transparency Masters, Blackline Masters, and Assessment Blackline Masters in the Unit Resource Guide are on the Teacher Resource CD.

Materials for the Teacher

Observational Assessment Record (Unit Resource Guide, Pages 7–8 and Teacher Resource CD)

Developing the Activity

Provide students with copies of the *Small Multiplication Tables* in the Generic Section so they can find any facts they need.

Part 1. Writing Multiplication Stories

Students will write stories to represent two-digit by one-digit multiplication problems. To begin, write a one-digit by one-digit multiplication problem on the board, e.g., 4×8, and ask the children to write and illustrate a story to represent it. (They did this type of work in the activity *Multiplication Stories* from Unit 3 *Exploring Multiplication* and should be familiar with it.) Here is an example story for 4×8:

There were 4 shirts, and each shirt had 8 buttons. The total number of buttons on the shirts was $4 \times 8 = 32$. (See Figure 3.)

Next, write a one-digit by two-digit problem on the board, e.g., 4×26, and ask students to write a story for it. These stories will be similar to the first ones, except for the size of the numbers. Ask students to illustrate their stories and to solve the multiplication problem. Encourage them to think of their own methods. Have children explain their methods to the class. Below are some methods they might use for 4×26:

1. 4×26 is $26 + 26 + 26 + 26$. I'll break apart each 26 to get $20 + 20 + 20 + 20 + 6 + 6 + 6 + 6 = 104$.

2. 26 is $25 + 1$. I know that $2 \times 25 = 50$, so I double that to get $4 \times 25 = 100$. Then, I add 4×1 and get 104.

3. If I think about money, 26¢ is 25¢ + 1¢. I know that 4 quarters are $1.00 and that 4 pennies are 4¢. So, 4×26¢ is $1.04. That is the same as 104¢, so $4 \times 26 = 104$.

4. $4 \times 26 = 4 \times 10 + 4 \times 10 + 4 \times 6$
   $= 40 + 40 + 24$
   $= 104$

5. $4 \times 26 = 4 \times 20 + 4 \times 6$
   $= 80 + 24$
   $= 104$

Figure 3: *4 shirts, each with 8 buttons, have $4 \times 8 = 32$ buttons*

Student Guide - Page 290

 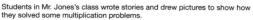

More Multiplication Stories

Students in Mr. Jones's class wrote stories and drew pictures to show how they solved some multiplication problems.

Here is Peter's story for the problem 4 × 26:

> A farmer had 4 chicken pens. Each held 26 chickens. How many chickens did he have in all?

Here is Peter's solution to the problem 4 × 26:

> 26 = 25 + 1. First, I find 4 × 25. To do that, I double 25 to get 50. I double that and get 100. I know that 4 × 1 is 4. So, 4 × 26 = 100 + 4 = 104.

Peter decided to change his story so that it matched the solution to his problem. Here is his new story and his picture:

> A farmer had 4 pens. Each held 25 brown chickens and 1 red chicken. How many chickens did he have in all?

Peter's Story

```
BBBBBBBBBB        BBBBBBBBBB        BBBBBBBBBB
BBBBBBBBBB        BBBBBBBBBB        BBBBBBBBBB
BBBBB             BBBBB             BBBBB
R                 R                 R
```

```
BBBBBBBBBB
BBBBBBBBBB
BBBBB
R
```

4 × 26 = 4 × 25 + 4 × 1
Brown   Red
Chickens   Chickens

290 SG · Grade 3 · Unit 19 · Lesson 2   More Multiplication Stories

Student Guide - Page 291

Here is Libby's story for the problem 72 × 3.

> 72 children at my brother's preschool have tricycles. How many wheels are on the tricycles?

Here is Libby's solution to the problem 72 × 3:

> 72 = 70 + 2. 70 × 3 is the same as 3 × 7 tens. That's 21 tens, which equal 210. 2 × 3 = 6. So, 72 × 3 = 210 + 6 = 216.

Libby changed her story to match her solution to the problem and drew a picture:

> 70 families in my brother's preschool had tricycles. Then, 2 more children got tricycles for their birthdays. How many wheels are on all the tricycles?

Preschool

70 tricycles

2 more tricycles

72 × 3 = 70 × 3 + 2 × 3
wheels on   wheels on
old tricycles   new tricycles

To solve 72 × 3, Libby broke 72 into 7 tens and 2 ones.

More Multiplication Stories   SG · Grade 3 · Unit 19 · Lesson 2 291

Part 2. Break-apart Products and Their Matching Stories

Many of the ways students solve their multiplication problems will involve breaking numbers apart into sums of easier products as in methods 2 through 5 above. Ask students to read Peter's story and solution to 4 × 26 on the *More Multiplication Stories* Activity Pages in the *Student Guide.* Point out that he revised his story to reflect the way he broke apart the numbers in his solution.

Here is an example of another way a student might revise a story to match a partition used in a solution. Suppose the student used method 4 above to solve 4 × 26 and that his or her story was, "There were 4 packages, and each held 26 popsicles. How many popsicles were there in all?" This story could be revised to match the partitioning of 26 into 10 + 10 + 6 as follows: "There were 4 boxes. Each held 10 cherry popsicles, 10 grape popsicles, and 6 orange popsicles. How many popsicles were there in all?"

Choose a few solutions that the class wrote for 4 × 26 and that involve breaking numbers apart. Have the class help to revise the corresponding stories so that they match the way the numbers were broken apart. Not all of the stories will be good candidates for revising in this way since they were not written with that goal in mind. When children write multiplication stories later in this activity, they can keep revision needs in mind.

Part 3. Breaking Factors into Tens and Ones

After discussing various ways to multiply, tell students that you would like them to focus on a particular way to break apart products at this time: partitioning factors into tens and ones. This is important practice since this partition is used in the paper-and-pencil multiplication algorithm.

The *More Multiplication Stories* Activity Pages continue with two stories—Libby's story for 72 × 3 and Alex's story for 63 × 4—which involve partitioning one factor into tens and ones. You can discuss these with the class. Here is another example problem you can use with the class:

6 × 53. There were 6 buses, and each had 50 passengers. Then, 3 more passengers got on each bus. How many passengers were there altogether? 6 × 50 + 6 × 3 = 300 + 18 = 318.

Figure 4: *6 × 53 passengers*

TIMS Tip

To help students think of stories, ask the class to brainstorm situations that might involve multiplying big numbers. Some examples include fish in whales' stomachs, animals in pens, people on trains, food in boxes, aliens on planets, cubic centimeters in glasses of water, moons around planets, and so on.

Continue writing and illustrating stories for several more two-digit by one-digit multiplication problems, first as a class and then individually when the students are ready. The stories should have a common theme of splitting groups into smaller groups of tens and ones. These stories should allow children to represent the arithmetic process used to solve multiplication problems in a way that is meaningful to them. In the past, we have often suggested that students use pictures and manipulatives to help them solve problems. In this case, drawing pictures should help them see why a particular way of solving multiplication problems—breaking apart products into tens and ones—makes sense. Creating a number sentence for their pictures will help students connect the arithmetic process they use to standard symbols.

Alex solved the problem 63 × 4 by breaking 63 into tens and ones. He used a computer to draw his picture. Notice that Alex's story matches the way he solved the problem. He broke 63 into 60 + 3. He solved 60 × 4 and 3 × 4. Then, he added the pieces.

Problem: 63 × 4

Old horses

60 horses wear   60 × 4 = 240 shoes

New horses

3 horses wear   3 × 4 = 12 shoes

63 horses wear   240 + 12 = 252 shoes ANSWER

Story: There were 60 horses on a farm. The farmer bought 3 more horses. Every horse wore 4 horseshoes. How many shoes did they wear altogether?

292 **SG · Grade 3 · Unit 19 · Lesson 2**   **More Multiplication Stories**

Student Guide - Page 292

Student Guide - Page 293

Student Guide - Page 294

In the Solving Problems Tyrone's Way section on the *More Multiplication Stories* Activity Pages, students are presented with eight two-digit by one-digit multiplication problems to solve. As a means of organizing their work, students are asked to model their work in the same way that Tyrone solved 5 × 37. First, they should write the problem at the top of the page. Then, they should divide their solutions into four parts: products to add, calculations, story, and picture. Their answers should be clearly indicated on their work.

Part 4. An Algorithm for Multiplication (Maria's Way)

After the students have solved many problems, introduce the paper-and-pencil multiplication algorithm shown in the Solving Problems Maria's Way section in the *Student Guide*.

```
  37    ⟶    30 + 7      step 1
× 4
  28    ⟵    4 × 7       step 2
+ 120   ⟵    4 × 30      step 3
  148               answer
```

This algorithm, called the *all-partials algorithm,* allows students to record all partial products. By having students record all of the intermediate products, they should develop a solid understanding of the algorithm. Students practice using this algorithm in *Questions 9–16.*

It is important that students check whether their answers are reasonable after any paper-and-pencil or calculator calculation. Sometimes, computed answers are ridiculously incorrect and a simple mental estimate will catch the error. For example, a child might estimate that the answer to 37 × 4 should be a little less than 160 since 40 × 4 = 160. If he or she had a computed answer of 148, this would be reasonable. Students should develop the important habit of checking whether their answers make sense.

Content Note

Changing the order in which the partial products are recorded in the all-partials algorithm does not change the answer. For example, when multiplying 37 × 4, one can record the 120 before the 28:

```
    37
  ×  4
   120
  +  28
   148
```

Suggestions for Teaching the Lesson

Math Facts

DPP Bit E asks students to complete a multiplication table for the last six facts. Task H develops strategies for the last six facts using skip counting.

Homework and Practice

- DPP Bit C provides addition and subtraction practice with money. Task D asks students to draw a picture for a multiplication problem involving a fraction. Items F and I are sets of word problems. Bit G develops mental math skills. Task J asks students to compare rectangles and squares.

- After students have worked through the problems in the *Student Guide* sections Solving Problems Tyrone's Way and Solving Problems Maria's Way, they can do the Homework section. Have students take home their *Small Multiplication Tables* from the Generic Section.

- Home Practice Part 2 provides further practice with addition, subtraction, and multiplication computation.

Answers for Part 2 of the Home Practice can be found in the Answer Key at the end of this lesson and at the end of this unit.

Name _____ Date _____

Unit 19: Home Practice

Part 1

Tell whether the sum of each is more than 600, less than 600, or equal to 600.

1. 300 + 300 _____
2. 318 + 264 _____
3. 268 + 295 _____
4. 329 + 282 _____
5. 240 + 360 _____
6. 363 + 302 _____

Fill in the blanks below so each number sentence equals 1000.

7. _____ + _____ + 300 = 1000
8. _____ + 150 + _____ = 1000
9. 335 + _____ + _____ = 1000

Part 2

1.	2.	3.	4.	5.	6.
79 + 69	979 − 430	75 × 4	32 × 9	60 × 4	83 × 7

7. Find two 3-digit numbers whose sum is 251. _____

8. Find two numbers whose difference is 79. _____

***Discovery Assignment Book* - Page 268**

Daily Practice and Problems: Tasks & Challenge for Lesson 2

D. Task: Multiplication Story $8 \times \frac{1}{4}$
(URG p. 12)

Write a story and draw a picture about $8 \times \frac{1}{4}$.

Write a number sentence on your picture.

F. Challenge: Making Change
(URG p. 13)

Beth asked for her allowance of $1.70 in nickels and dimes. Her parents gave her $1.00 using one kind of coin and $.70 using the other coin.

1. How many nickels did Beth possibly get? How many dimes?

2. Beth said, "I wanted the same number of nickels as dimes." Is this possible? If so, how many nickels? How many dimes? If not, why?

H. Task: Skip Counting
(URG p. 14)

1. Skip count by 4s to 100. Say the numbers quietly to yourself. Write the numbers.

2. Skip count by 8s until you pass 100. Say the numbers quietly to yourself. Write the numbers.

3. Circle the numbers in your lists that are products of (answers to) the last six facts:

4×6	4×7	4×8
6×7	6×8	7×8

4. How could you use skip counting to find these facts?

5. Which of the last six facts is not circled? Why not?

J. Task: Squares and Rectangles
(URG p. 15)

1. Draw a square. Then, write what a square is.

2. Draw a rectangle. Then, write what a rectangle is.

3. What is the difference between squares and rectangles?

4. Is a square a rectangle?

5. Is a rectangle a square?

Suggestions for Teaching the Lesson (continued)

Assessment

- Ask students to solve the problem 4 × 34 representing their work Tyrone's Way. This activity can be used to assess students' abilities to create stories for multiplication sentences and explain their solution strategies. Record your observations using the *Observational Assessment Record.*

- Use the homework problems on the *More Multiplication Stories* Activity Pages to assess students' understanding of the paper-and-pencil algorithm.

Software Connection

- *Kid Pix* or other drawing software.

  If you have access to computers that are equipped with a drawing program, students can illustrate their multiplication stories using computers. Josh's picture on the *More Multiplication Stories* Activity Pages was drawn using *Kid Pix.*

- *National Library of Virtual Manipulatives* website (http://matti.usu.edu). This website allows students to work with manipulatives including rectangle multiplication that models the all-partials algorithm.

AT A GLANCE

Math Facts and Daily Practice and Problems

DPP Bit E and Task H provide practice with the last six multiplication facts. Items C, D, F, G, and I provide computation practice. Task J asks students to compare rectangles and squares.

Part 1. Writing Multiplication Stories

1. Write a one-digit by one-digit multiplication problem on the board, such as 4 × 8.
2. Students write and illustrate a story to represent it.
3. Write a one-digit by two-digit problem on the board, such as 4 × 26.
4. Students write stories, illustrate their stories, and solve the problems using their own methods.
5. Students explain their methods to the class.

AT A GLANCE

Part 2. Break-apart Products and Their Matching Stories

1. Students read Peter's story and solution to 4×26 on the *More Multiplication Stories* Activity Pages in the *Student Guide.*
2. Point out that Peter revised his story to reflect the way he broke apart the numbers in his solution.
3. Provide another example showing how to revise a story to match a partition used in a solution.
4. Choose a few solutions that involve breaking numbers apart that the class wrote for 4×26.
5. The class helps to revise the stories so that they match the way the numbers were broken apart.

Part 3. Breaking Factors into Tens and Ones

1. Focus on breaking apart products by partitioning factors into tens and ones.
2. Read and discuss Libby's and Alex's stories on the *More Multiplication Stories* Activity Pages.
3. Students write and illustrate stories for two-digit multiplication problems, as a class and individually.
4. Students use pictures to solve the problems. They create number sentences for their pictures.
5. In the Solving Problems Tyrone's Way section in the *Student Guide* students solve two-digit by one-digit multiplication problems. Students divide their solutions into four parts: products to add, calculations, story, and picture. *(Questions 1–8)*

Part 4. An Algorithm for Multiplication (Maria's Way)

1. Introduce the multiplication algorithm shown in the Solving Problems Maria's Way section in the *Student Guide.*
2. Students practice using this algorithm in *Questions 9–16.*
3. Encourage students to check whether their answers are reasonable.

Homework

1. Assign Home Practice Part 2.
2. Assign the Homework section in the *Student Guide.*

Assessment

1. Ask students to solve the problem 4×34 representing their work Tyrone's Way. Record your observations using the *Observational Assessment Record.*
2. Use the homework problems in the *Student Guide* to assess students' understanding of the paper-and-pencil algorithm.

Notes:

Student Guide

Questions 1–16 (SG p. 294)

Stories and pictures will vary.

1. 3×54
   $3 \times 50 = 150$
   $3 \times 4 = 12$
   $3 \times 54 = 150 + 12 = 162$

2. 31×8
   $30 \times 8 = 240$
   $1 \times 8 = 8$
   $31 \times 8 = 240 + 8 = 248$

3. 5×67
   $5 \times 60 = 300$
   $5 \times 7 = 35$
   $5 \times 67 = 300 + 35 = 335$

4. 45×6
   $40 \times 6 = 240$
   $5 \times 6 = 30$
   $45 \times 6 = 240 + 30 = 270$

5. 4×28
   $4 \times 20 = 80$
   $4 \times 8 = 32$
   $4 \times 28 = 80 + 32 = 112$

6. 62×5
   $60 \times 5 = 300$
   $2 \times 5 = 10$
   $62 \times 5 = 300 + 10 = 310$

7. 58×5
   $50 \times 5 = 250$
   $8 \times 5 = 40$
   $58 \times 5 = 250 + 40 = 290$

8. 7×36
   $7 \times 30 = 210$
   $7 \times 6 = 42$
   $7 \times 36 = 210 + 42 = 252$

9.
$$
\begin{array}{r}
21 \\
\times\ 8 \\
\hline
8 \\
+\ 160 \\
\hline
168
\end{array}
$$

10.
$$
\begin{array}{r}
84 \\
\times\ 3 \\
\hline
12 \\
+\ 240 \\
\hline
252
\end{array}
$$

11.
$$
\begin{array}{r}
75 \\
\times\ 3 \\
\hline
15 \\
+\ 210 \\
\hline
225
\end{array}
$$

12.
$$
\begin{array}{r}
61 \\
\times\ 5 \\
\hline
5 \\
+\ 300 \\
\hline
305
\end{array}
$$

13.
$$
\begin{array}{r}
46 \\
\times\ 8 \\
\hline
48 \\
+\ 320 \\
\hline
368
\end{array}
$$

14.
$$
\begin{array}{r}
52 \\
\times\ 9 \\
\hline
18 \\
+\ 450 \\
\hline
468
\end{array}
$$

15.
$$
\begin{array}{r}
34 \\
\times\ 6 \\
\hline
24 \\
+\ 180 \\
\hline
204
\end{array}
$$

16.
$$
\begin{array}{r}
91 \\
\times\ 5 \\
\hline
5 \\
+\ 450 \\
\hline
455
\end{array}
$$

Homework (SG p. 294)

Questions 1–10

1. 174
2. 207
3. 117
4. 306
5. 316
6. 126
7. 408
8. 424
9. 210
10. 111; stories and pictures will vary.

Discovery Assignment Book

**Home Practice (DAB p. 268)

Part 2

Questions 1–8

1. 148
2. 549
3. 300
4. 288
5. 240
6. 581
7. Answers will vary. One example is $111 + 140 = 251$
8. Answers will vary. One example is $164 - 85 = 79$

*Answers and/or discussion are included in the Lesson Guide.

**Answers for all the Home Practice in the *Discovery Assignment Book* are at the end of the unit.

LESSON GUIDE

Making Groups

Estimated Class Sessions: 1

Students consider the number of groups of equal size that can be made from various numbers of objects. The groupings involve divisions of numbers between 25 and 50, many of which cannot be solved using a simple reversal of multiplication facts. Particular attention is given to remainders.

Key Content

- Dividing a set of objects into equal-size groups (with remainders).
- Representing division problems using drawings and manipulatives.
- Writing number sentences for division situations.
- Dividing two-digit numbers.
- Investigating patterns involving remainders.
- Interpreting remainders.

Daily Practice and Problems: Bit for Lesson 3

K. Double, Double Again (URG p. 15)

Solve the following problems.

1. $6 \times 2 =$ 2. $6 \times 4 =$

3. $8 \times 2 =$ 4. $8 \times 4 =$

5. $7 \times 2 =$ 6. $14 \times 2 =$

7. $7 \times 4 =$ 8. $14 \times 4 =$

9. $7 \times 8 =$

DPP Task is on page 42. Suggestions for using the DPPs are on page 42.

Curriculum Sequence

Before This Unit

Making Groups. Students divided objects into equal-size groups with remainders in Grade 3 Unit 3 Lesson 4 *Making Teams.*

Materials List

Print Materials for Students

	Math Facts and Daily Practice and Problems	Activity	Homework	Written Assessment
Student Book — Discovery Assignment Book			Home Practice Part 3 Page 269	
Teacher Resources — Facts Resource Guide ⊙	DPP Item 19K			
Teacher Resources — Unit Resource Guide	DPP Items K–L Pages 15–16 ⊙			DPP Item L *Multiplication Story 38 × 4* Page 16 ⊙
Teacher Resources — Generic Section ⊙		*Four-column Data Table,* 3 to 4 per student		*Four-column Data Table,* 1 per student

⊙ available on Teacher Resource CD

All Transparency Masters, Blackline Masters, and Assessment Blackline Masters in the Unit Resource Guide are on the Teacher Resource CD.

Supplies for Each Student

50 connecting cubes

Materials for the Teacher

Observational Assessment Record (Unit Resource Guide, Pages 7–8 and Teacher Resource CD)

Developing the Activity

This activity is similar to the activity *Making Teams* from Unit 3 *Exploring Multiplication.* However, this activity involves larger numbers and emphasizes division rather than multiplication.

On the board, write a number between 25 and 50, that will represent the number of objects to be divided into groups. (In the following discussion, 30 is used as an example.) Ask students to suggest a number to represent the size of the groups to be made. (We will use 7 as an example.) Ask the class how many groups of that size can be made from the objects and how many will be left over.

To help them think about the problem, students can divide collections of connecting cubes into groups or they can write Xs in rows to represent groups of objects. For example, if the number of objects is 30 and the number in each group is 7, they can write 4 rows of 7 Xs, with 2 left over:

$$\begin{array}{l}
\text{X X X X X X X} \\
\text{X X X X X X X} \\
\text{X X X X X X X} \\
\text{X X X X X X X} \\
\text{X X} \qquad\qquad 30 \div 7 = 4 \text{ R2}
\end{array}$$

Ask for another number for the size of a group. Tell students to find out how many groups they can now make of that size using the new group size. Continue in this manner, investigating several different group sizes. Ask students to record their findings on the *Four-column Data Table* or in a similar one they draw on their own paper. They should record the number of objects to be divided into groups at the top of the table. After a discussion of several groupings of 30 objects, their tables should look like Figure 5.

The number to be divided into groups is 30.

Size of Groups	Number of Groups	Number left Over	Number Sentence
7	4	2	$30 \div 7 = 4$ R2
2	15	0	$30 \div 2 = 15$
13	2	4	$30 \div 13 = 2$ R4
8	3	6	$30 \div 8 = 3$ R6
20	1	10	$30 \div 20 = 1$ R10

Figure 5: *A sample data table for groupings of 30 objects*

During your discussion, make use of the various ways to phrase division questions:

- *How many 7s are in 30?*
- *What is 30 divided by 7?*
- *How many times does 7 go into 30?*

After students have considered several different group sizes, ask them to write down any patterns they find. Below are some possible responses:

1. The number left over is always less than the size of the group.
2. As you make the group size bigger, the number of groups gets smaller.
3. If the group size is more than half the number of objects, you will have only one group.

Repeat this activity several times with different numbers of objects and ask students to continue to look for patterns.

Suggestions for Teaching the Lesson

Math Facts

DPP Bit K provides practice with multiplication facts and using doubles.

Homework and Practice

- Ask students to complete a table for 56 like the one they did in the lesson. Ask students to divide this number into various size groups using a *Four-column Data Table.*
- Home Practice Part 3 asks students to review measuring and finding area and perimeter of different two-dimensional shapes.

Answers for Part 3 of the Home Practice can be found in the Answer Key at the end of this lesson and at the end of this unit.

Assessment

- Ask students to complete a table like the one they did in the activity for a different number between 20 and 50. Observe students' abilities to write number sentences for division situations and interpret remainders. Record your observations on the *Observational Assessment Record.*
- Use DPP Task L *Multiplication Story 38 × 4* as an assessment.

Daily Practice and Problems:
Task for Lesson 3

L. Task: Multiplication Story 38 × 4
(URG p. 16)

Solve 38 × 4. Write a story and draw a picture to match your solution.

Name _____ Date _____

Part 3

1. Draw a rectangle, a pentagon, and a hexagon on paper. Draw the pentagon with the largest area, and the rectangle with the smallest area. You do not have to find the exact area of each shape. Use a ruler to make your drawings.

2. Michael measured his height. He said to his mom, "I am 48." She said, "No, you're not. You're 8!" How could Michael and his mother have avoided this misunderstanding?

   _____

3. Measure and record the perimeter of a table top in your home. Draw a picture of the table you measured and show the length of each side. Remember to include the units.

   _____

4. List the following measurements in order from shortest to longest.
   5 inches, 5 meters, 5 cm

Part 4

1. Write a story and draw a picture about $\frac{1}{4} \times 20$ on a sheet of paper. Write a number sentence on your picture.

2. How many 10-gram masses would it take to balance a 120-gram object?

3. A +6 mathhopper takes 60 hops, starting at 0. Where does it land? If it takes 63 hops, where does it land?

4. A. 96   B. 64   C. 40   D. 47
      × 2   × 8   × 7   × 3

MULTIPLICATION AND DIVISION PROBLEMS   DAB · Grade 3 · Unit 19 269

Discovery Asignment Book - Page 269

AT A GLANCE

Math Facts and Daily Practice and Problems

DPP Bit K provides practice with using doubles to solve multiplication problems and Task L asks students to create a story and draw a picture for a multiplication problem.

Developing the Activity

1. On the board, write a number between 25 and 50 to represent the quantity of cubes to be divided.
2. Students decide how many they want in each group.
3. Students find how many groups and how many remain using cubes or drawings.
4. Students repeat the divisions with other group sizes and record the results and the division number sentences on a *Four-column Data Table.*
5. Students look for patterns in their tables.
6. Students repeat the activity with other group sizes.

Homework

1. Assign Home Practice Part 3.
2. Ask students to complete a table for 56 like the one they completed in the lesson.

Assessment

1. Observe students' abilities to write number sentences for division situations and interpret remainders while they complete a table like the one in the lesson. Record observations on the *Observational Assessment Record.*
2. Use DPP Task L as an assessment.

Notes:

Discovery Assignment Book

**Home Practice (DAB p. 269)

Part 3

Questions 1–4

1. Check for size relationship as follows:

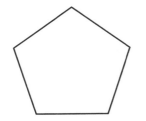

  The pentagon and hexagon do not have to be regular shapes. Their sides and angles may vary in size.

2. Answers will vary. However, students' explanations should include the idea that Michael and his mother are confused because neither of them remembered to give the proper unit of measurement. Michael should have said he was 48 inches tall and his mother should have said he was 8 years old.

3. Accept any reasonable answer. The total measurement should equal the sum of the sides. Lengths should be given in inches or centimeters.

4. 5 cm, 5 inches, 5 meters

*Answers and/or discussion are included in the Lesson Guide.

**Answers for all the Home Practice in the *Discovery Assignment Book* are at the end of the unit.

LESSON GUIDE 4

Solving Problems with Division

Estimated Class Sessions: **3**

Students solve multiplication and division word problems, including some division problems that involve remainders. They also solve challenging multistep problems whose solutions use both multiplication and division.

Key Content

- Solving multiplication and division problems and explaining the reasoning.
- Interpreting remainders.
- Solving multistep word problems.

Daily Practice and Problems: Bits for Lesson 4

M. Today, Tonight, or Tomorrow?
(URG p. 16)

1. What time will it be 4 hours from now?
2. What time will it be $6\frac{1}{3}$ hours from now?
3. What time will it be 8 hours from now?
4. What time will it be $12\frac{1}{4}$ hours from now?

O. Some More Sums (URG p. 17)

Add 27 to each of the numbers below.

65   189   2977

Q. Multiplication Quiz: The Last Six Facts (URG p. 17)

A. $8 \times 6 =$ B. $6 \times 4 =$

C. $4 \times 7 =$ D. $7 \times 8 =$

E. $6 \times 7 =$ F. $8 \times 4 =$

DPP Tasks and Challenge are on page 49. Suggestions for using the DPPs are on page 48.

Curriculum Sequence

Before This Unit

Division with Remainders. In Grade 3 Unit 7 Lesson 4 *Birthday Party* and Lesson 5 *Money Jar,* students solved division problems and wrote number sentences for their solutions. They interpreted remainders, including remainders resulting from division using a calculator. In Unit 11 Lesson 6 *Division in Lizardland,* students solved word problems involving division and investigated division involving zero.

Materials List

Print Materials for Students

		Math Facts and Daily Practice and Problems	Activity	Homework	Written Assessment
Student Books	**Student Guide**		*Solving Problems with Division* Pages 295–297	*Solving Problems with Division* Homework Section Page 298	
	Discovery Assignment Book			Home Practice Part 4 Page 269	
Teacher Resources	**Facts Resource Guide** ⊙	DPP Item 19P & 19Q			DPP Item 19Q *Multiplication Quiz: The Last Six Facts*
	Unit Resource Guide	DPP Items M–R Pages 16–18 ⊙			DPP Item Q *Multiplication Quiz: The Last Six Facts* Page 17 ⊙ and *Multiplication and Division* Page 51, 1 per student
	Generic Section ⊙		*Small Multiplication Tables,* 1 table per student		

⊙ *available on Teacher Resource CD*

All Transparency Masters, Blackline Masters, and Assessment Blackline Masters in the Unit Resource Guide are on the Teacher Resource CD.

Supplies for Each Student

base-ten pieces, optional
connecting cubes, optional
calculators, optional

Materials for the Teacher

Observational Assessment Record (Unit Resource Guide, Pages 7–8 and Teacher Resource CD)
Individual Assessment Record Sheet (Teacher Implementation Guide, Assessment section and Teacher Resource CD)

Developing the Activity

Ask students to solve *Questions 1–7* on the *Solving Problems with Division* Activity Pages. Some are multiplication problems and some are division problems. Many of the division problems involve three-digit dividends. Students can use any method that makes sense to them to solve these problems. No formal division algorithm is introduced at this time.

These problems can be solved in a variety of ways. Encourage students to share their strategies for solving these problems. Students may:

- Use repeated addition or subtraction to find a solution.
- Use connecting cubes or base-ten pieces to model the process.
- Write a number sentence and use a calculator.
- Estimate a solution and then try a variety of ways to find it.

Discuss students' strategies and encourage them to brainstorm other ways that they might have solved the problems. Students should be encouraged to try a variety of strategies for each problem. Trying multiple strategies will verify their solutions while helping them prepare for later problem-solving situations.

Questions 8–12 are division problems with remainders. The class should discuss the different ways that remainders are treated. In *Question 8,* division gives $250 \div 60 = 4$ R10. Since the remainder 10 represents the number of children who are left after four buses are filled and since these children still need to ride a bus, the answer should be rounded up to the next whole number of buses: 5. In *Question 9,* division gives $\$1.00 \div \$.30 = 3$ R$.10; the remainder $.10 is extra money. Since it is not enough to buy a pencil, it must be dropped (or put back into Julia's pocket). In *Question 10,* division gives $21 \div 4 = 5$ R1. The remainder 1 is an extra pizza. It can be cut into fourths so that each class gets one-fourth. Thus, the answer is $5\frac{1}{4}$ pizzas. *Question 11* asks students to divide 23 students into four groups. $23 \div 4 = 5$ R3. The three remaining students are added to three groups, so that there are three groups of six students and only one group of five students. These problems give different ways to deal with remainders: round up, round down, express as a fraction, and distribute the leftovers as equally as possible.

Solving Problems with Division

Story Problems

Solve the following problems. For each problem, explain how you found your solution.

1. We bought 12 packages of juice boxes. Each package had 6 boxes. How many boxes did we buy?

2. Juan bought 200 marbles. Each bag contained 50 marbles. How many bags of marbles did he buy?

3. Juan divided his 200 marbles equally among himself and his four friends. How many marbles did each of them get?

4. For her birthday, Anne wants to invite six friends to go skating with her. If tickets cost $1.50 per person, how much will it cost for Anne and her friends to skate?

5. Each cupcake box holds a half dozen cupcakes. How many boxes are needed to hold 48 cupcakes?

6. Five children found $3.00 on the playground. When no one claimed it, the principal said they could share it equally. How much did each child get?

Multiply or Divide?

7. Look back over the problems you solved in Questions 1–6. Write number sentences for each one. Which problems have multiplication sentences and which have division sentences?

Student Guide - Page 295

Problems with Remainders

Each of the following problems involves division and remainders. For each problem, deal with the remainder in a way that makes sense for the question asked.

8. The 250 children from Johnson Elementary School were going on a field trip. Each bus could hold 60 children. How many buses would they need?

9. Julia earned $1.00 and wanted to spend it to buy some fancy pencils for school. If each pencil costs $.30, how many pencils could she buy?

10. The Johnson Elementary School ordered 21 pizzas for the 4 third-grade classes to share equally. How many pizzas did each class get?

11. The 23 students in a third-grade classroom were divided into four groups. Each group should be as close to the same size as possible. How many students were in each group?

Your Division Stories

12. Write your own stories to match the following division problems. Then, solve the problems. Include in your stories what happens to any remainders.
    A. $26 \div 5 = ?$
    B. $75 \div 10 = ?$
    C. $140 \div 2 = ?$

Student Guide - Page 296

The Bake Sale

Mrs. Joseph's class is planning a bake sale. Help them plan for it by solving the following problems and explaining how you got your answers. Some solutions might involve both multiplication and division.

13. Kate can make 3 dozen cupcakes for the bake sale. If she puts four cupcakes in each bag, how many bags of cupcakes will she have?

14. The class plans to buy cans of frozen lemonade. Each can makes 64 oz of lemonade. If they buy four cans, how many 6-oz cups can be filled?

15. George is going to make 64 brownies for the bake sale. If he puts 4 brownies in each bag and each bag sells for $.50, how much money will they make selling George's brownies?

16. Tess is going to make 90 crispy treats and divide them equally into 30 bags. The price for one bag of crispy treats is $.75.
   A. How much does one crispy treat cost?
   B. How much will they make if they sell all the crispy treats?

Solving Problems with Division   SG · Grade 3 · Unit 19 · Lesson 4   297

Student Guide - Page 297

Questions 13–16 are more challenging because they require more than one step.

Suggestions for Teaching the Lesson

Math Facts

Task P uses rectangles to practice multiplication facts.

Homework and Practice

- DPP Bit M provides practice with time. Challenge N asks students to solve problems using skip counting or multiplication. Bit O provides addition practice. Task R asks students to solve Lizardland problems involving money.

- Assign the Homework section in the *Student Guide.*

- Home Practice Part 4 asks students to solve problems involving multiplication.

Answers for Part 4 of the Home Practice can be found in the Answer Key at the end of this lesson and at the end of this unit.

Assessment

- DPP Bit Q is a quiz on the last six multiplication facts.

- Use the *Multiplication and Division* Assessment Blackline Master to assess students' abilities to multiply two-digit by one-digit numbers to solve problems involving multiplication and division. Allow students to use multiplication tables.

- Note students' abilities to solve multiplication and division problems and explain their reasoning on the *Observational Assessment Record.*

- Transfer appropriate Unit 19 observations to students' *Individual Assessment Record Sheets.*

Extension

Use your calendars from the *Multiples on the Calendar* activity to write division sentences. Students can chart the factors and the remainders for certain numbers. Encourage students to look for and discuss patterns in their calendars. Students may recognize that there is a relationship between multiplication and division sentences.

Homework

Solve the following problems.

1. $2 \times 8 = ?$
2. $9/3 = ?$
3. $6 \times 7 = ?$
4. $30 \div 5 = ?$
5. $28/4 = ?$
6. $7 \times 9 = ?$
7. $45 \div 5 = ?$
8. $24/6 = ?$
9. $64/8 = ?$
10. $13/1 = ?$
11. $10/2 = ?$
12. $3 \times 7 = ?$

13. A. Elly made one dozen sandwiches for a picnic with 3 of her friends. If the four girls want to share equally, how many sandwiches will each friend get?

   B. Elly's friend Emma brought a 64 oz pitcher of juice to share with the group. How much juice will each friend get?

   C. Elizabeth made 6 cupcakes to share with the group. How many cupcakes will each friend get?

14. Write a story problem to go with one of the multiplication problems in Questions 1–12.

15. Write a story problem to go with one of the division problems in Questions 1–12.

Student Guide - Page 298

Name _____ Date _____

Part 3

1. Draw a rectangle, a pentagon, and a hexagon on paper. Draw the pentagon with the largest area, and the rectangle with the smallest area. You do not have to find the exact area of each shape. Use a ruler to make your drawings.

2. Michael measured his height. He said to his mom, "I am 48." She said, "No, you're not. You're 8!" How could Michael and his mother have avoided this misunderstanding?

3. Measure and record the perimeter of a table top in your home. Draw a picture of the table you measured and show the length of each side. Remember to include the units.

4. List the following measurements in order from shortest to longest.
   5 inches, 5 meters, 5 cm

Part 4

1. Write a story and draw a picture about $\frac{1}{4} \times 20$ on a sheet of paper. Write a number sentence on your picture.

2. How many 10-gram masses would it take to balance a 120-gram object?

3. A +6 mathhopper takes 60 hops, starting at 0. Where does it land? If it takes 63 hops, where does it land?

4. A. $\begin{array}{r} 96 \\ \times\ 2 \\ \hline \end{array}$
    B. $\begin{array}{r} 64 \\ \times\ 8 \\ \hline \end{array}$
    C. $\begin{array}{r} 40 \\ \times\ 7 \\ \hline \end{array}$
    D. $\begin{array}{r} 47 \\ \times\ 3 \\ \hline \end{array}$

Discovery Assignment Book - Page 269

Daily Practice and Problems:
Tasks & Challenge for Lesson 4

N. Challenge: Mathhoppers on the Calculator (URG p. 16)

1. A +9 mathhopper starts at 2 and hops 15 times. Estimate where it lands.

2. Where does it land exactly? Tell how you know.

3. How many more hops does it need to take to reach 200?

P. Task: Rectangles and Products (URG p. 17)

1. Using *Centimeter Grid Paper,* draw all the rectangles you can make with 32 tiles.

2. Draw all the rectangles you can make with 24 tiles.

R. Task: Saturday at Lizardland (URG p. 18)

Use the Lizardland picture in your *Student Guide* from Unit 11 to solve the following problems.

1. On Saturday, in the first hour, 100 adults and 200 children came to Lizardland. How much was collected in ticket sales?

2. Last Saturday 600 adults and 1000 children came to Lizardland. How much was collected in ticket sales?

3. Fifty-nine members of the Jones family reunion came to Lizardland on Saturday. Forty-four family members were children. Fifteen were adults. How much did they pay to get in?

AT A GLANCE

Math Facts and Daily Practice and Problems

DPP Bit M provides practice with time. Items N, O, and R provide computation practice. Items P and Q practice and assess multiplication facts.

Developing the Activity

1. Students solve *Questions 1–7* on the *Solving Problems with Division* Activity Pages in the *Student Guide* using a variety of strategies. These problems involve multiplication and division.
2. Students brainstorm and discuss other ways to solve these problems.
3. Students solve *Questions 8–12* which involve division and remainders.
4. Students discuss what to do with the remainders in *Questions 8–11.*
5. Students solve *Questions 13–16* which involve more than one step.

Homework

1. Assign Home Practice Part 4.
2. Assign the homework problems on the *Solving Problems with Division* Activity Pages.

Assessment

1. DPP Bit Q is a quiz on the last six multiplication facts.
2. Assign the *Multiplication and Division* Assessment Blackline Master. Students should have multiplication tables available.
3. Note students' progress solving multiplication and division problems. Transfer appropriate Unit 19 *Observational Assessment Record* observations to students' *Individual Assessment Record Sheets*.

Name _____ Date _____

Multiplication and Division

1. Solve 28 x 3. Write a story and draw a picture to match your solution.

Solve the problems.

2. 15
   × 7
   ___

3. 30
   × 6
   ___

4. 42
   × 9
   ___

5. Four people can ride in each car on the roller coaster in Lizardland. How many cars will it take so that all 26 students from Mr. Carter's third grade can ride the roller coaster? Explain your reasoning.

Student Guide

Questions 1–16 (SG pp. 295–297)

Solution strategies will vary.

1. $12 \times 6 = 72$ boxes
2. $200 \div 50 = 4$ bags
3. $200 \div 5 = 40$ marbles
4. $\$1.50 \times 7 = \$10.50$
5. $48 \div 6 = 8$ boxes
6. $\$3.00 \div 5 = \$.60$
7. Answers may vary. For example, in Question 2, students could write either $50 \times 4 = 200$ or $200 \div 50 = 4$.
8. *5 buses
9. *3 pencils
10. *$5\frac{1}{4}$ pizzas
11. *Three groups had six students and one group had five students.
12. Answers will vary according to the stories written.

    Check to see that students treat the remainders in ways that match their stories.

For Questions 13–16 solution strategies will vary.

13. 9 bags
14. 42 R4; 42 cups
15. $8.00
16. **A.** $.25

    B. $22.50

Homework (SG p. 298)

Questions 1–15

1. 16	2. 3
3. 42	4. 6
5. 7	6. 63
7. 9	8. 4
9. 8	10. 13
11. 5	12. 21

13. **A.** $12 \div 4 = 3$ sandwiches per person

    B. $64 \div 4 = 16$ oz of juice per person

    C. $6 \div 4 = 1\frac{1}{2}$ cupcakes per person each or 1 cupcake each and 2 left over

14. Answers will vary.
15. Answers will vary.

*Answers and/or discussion are included in the Lesson Guide.

**Answers for all the Home Practice in the *Discovery Assignment Book* are at the end of the unit.

Discovery Assignment Book

**Home Practice (DAB p. 269)

Part 4

Questions 1–4

1. Answers will vary. The story should match the picture. Here is one story and illustration:

   Toni was having a party for twenty people. He knew each person would eat $\frac{1}{4}$ of a super deluxe pizza. How many pizzas does Toni need to order for the party?

$$\frac{1}{4} \times 20 = 5$$

2. 12 10-gram masses
3. 360; 378
4. **A.** 192
   B. 512
   C. 280
   D. 141

Unit Resource Guide

Multiplication and Division (URG p. 51)

Questions 1–5

1. 84; Stories and pictures will vary.
2. 105
3. 180
4. 378
5. $26 \div 4 = 6$ R2; It will take 7 cars for all the students to ride. Six cars will have four students and they need one more car for the two remaining students.

---

*Answers and/or discussion are included in the Lesson Guide.

**Answers for all the Home Practice in the *Discovery Assignment Book* are at the end of the unit.

Discovery Assignment Book

Part 1

Questions 1–9 (DAB p. 268)

1. equal
2. less than
3. less than
4. more than
5. equal
6. more than
7. Answers will vary. One example is
   400 + 300 + 300 = 1000
8. Answers will vary. One example is
   350 + 150 + 500 = 1000
9. Answers will vary. One example is
   335 + 165 + 500 = 1000

Part 2

Questions 1–8 (DAB p. 268)

1. 148
2. 549
3. 300
4. 288
5. 240
6. 581
7. Answers will vary. One example is
   111 + 140 = 251
8. Answers will vary. One example is
   164 − 85 = 79

Part 3

Questions 1–4 (DAB p. 269)

1. Check for size relationship as follows:

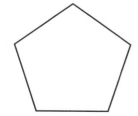

The pentagon and hexagon do not have to be regular shapes. Their sides and angles may vary in size.

2. Answers will vary. However, students' explanations should include the idea that Michael and his mother are confused because neither of them remembered to give the proper unit of measurement. Michael should have said he was 48 inches tall and his mother should have said he was 8 years old.

3. Accept any reasonable answer. The total measurement should equal the sum of the sides. Lengths should be given in inches or centimeters.

4. 5 cm, 5 inches, 5 meters

Part 4

Questions 1–4 (DAB p. 269)

1. Answers will vary. The story should match the picture. Here is one story and illustration:

   Toni was having a party for twenty people. He knew each person would eat $\frac{1}{4}$ of a super deluxe pizza. How many pizzas does Toni need to order for the party?

$$\frac{1}{4} \times 20 = 5$$

2. 12 10-gram masses
3. 360; 378
4. **A.** 192
   B. 512
   C. 280
   D. 141

*Answers and/or discussion are included in the Lesson Guide.